THE VILLAGE SCHOOL

A play by

RON PERRY

BASED ON THE FAIRACRE NOVELS

BY MISS READ

Copyright © Ron Perry and the Estate of Dora Saint (Miss Read)
2024

No part of this publication may lawfully be reproduced in any form or by any means – photocopying, typescript, recording (including video-recording), manuscript, electronic, mechanical, or otherwise – or be transmitted or stored in a retrieval system without prior permission.

The publication of these plays does not imply that it is necessarily available for performance by amateurs or professionals, either in the British Isles or overseas.

All business negotiations for the play shall be conducted through Ron Perry Plays (ronperryplays@outlook.com),
the sole agents for the play.

Prior to using the incidental music specified in this play, the place of the performance must be licensed by the Performing Rights Society

A note from 'Miss Read's' daughter...

Village School was the first Miss Read book, and made far more impact than anyone had anticipated, with excellent reviews and a great deal of publicity. Later, it was a set book for CSE English, which is where Ron Perry first encountered the books.

It was commissioned by Michael Joseph Ltd, and on hearing that it should be 70,000 words long, my mother's initial reaction was that she couldn't do it. Her account of this interview is entertainingly told in *Mrs Griffin Sends Her Love,* the compilation of her earlier work that her long-time editor, Jenny Dereham, and I managed to finish for publication in Dora's centenary year, 2013.

Ron's first adaptation of a Miss Read book was *Thrush Green* in 2017. The action of the book takes place in one day – the day of the annual May fair – and the resulting play was magical. It was performed in a transparent marquee in a buttercup field, in May, and the sun went down during the performance.

This play has an equally inspired staging, within the schoolroom, with the audience almost part of the class. Ron has more than done justice to the Miss Read books with his adaptations, and I know that my mother would have been delighted with the results. She would also have been very pleased that some of John Goodall's illustrations were used in the sets, as she always felt that his work was almost a partnership and did so much to enhance the books.

To have Miss Read's novels expanded in this most sensitive and attractive way is a delight, and I hope that in due course the plays may become known to a wider audience.

Jill Saint

Cast

Mrs Pringle (The School Cleaner)

Miss Read (Headmistress)

Mr Willet (School Caretaker)

Miss Clare (Infant Teacher)

Ernest (Pupil)

Anne (Pupil)

Edna (Pupil, Non-Speaking)

Sylvia (Pupil, Non-Speaking)

Reverend Gerald Partridge

Linda (Pupil)

Miss Pitt (The County Needlework Inspector)

Dr Martin

Mr Roberts (Local Farmer and School Manager)

Mrs Lamb (School Manager)

Miss Quinn (School Manager)

Minnie Pringle

Mr Salisbury (Caxley Educational Officer)

Mrs Benson (A Villager)

Mrs Amy James

This play was first performed on 22nd May 2024 at Redlynch Village Hall, Wiltshire by Redlynch Players with Fordingbridge Players, with the following cast and production team:

Mrs Pringle	Sarah Newman
Miss Read	Gina Hodsman
Mr Willet	Graham Collier
Miss Clare	Jill Saunders
Ernest	Mark Newman
Anne	Annie Mitchell
Edna	Emma Tanner
Rosie	Debbie Newcombe
Sylvia	Nicki Salmond
Nellie	Ali Silver
Linda	Sue Ball
Reverend Gerald Partridge	Andy Harrison-King
Miss Pitt	Annie Mitchell
Dr Martin	Lloyd Perry
Mr Roberts	Lloyd Perry
Mrs Lamb	Debbie Newcombe
Miss Quinn	Annie Mitchell
Minnie Pringle	Nicki Salmond
Mr Salisbury	Mark Newman
Mrs Benson	Sue Ball
Mrs Amy James	Nicki Salmond
Chorister	Ali Silver

Director	Ron Perry
Producer	Lloyd Perry
Stage Management & Props	Mark Newman
	Marilyn Perry
Lighting, Sound Effects and Music	Charlotte Eardley
	Roger Coles

Pre-performance: *Village soundscape; children playing, farm animals, dogs, rooks, etc....*

Act One

Scene One

Music: *"Flocks a Mile Wide" by Christopher Tin*

We are in Fairacre Village School, near Newbury, Berkshire.

The blackboard states Monday 5th September 1955.

We discover **Mrs Pringle**, *the school cleaner who is sixtyish, stout and sour, scrubbing the school room floor on her knees. She sings (not in tune) in a booming contralto voice, "Oft in danger, oft in woe".* **Miss Read** *enters. She is a mousy woman in her fifties.*

Miss Read (*Talking to the audience*) I have been headmistress of the tiny school in the lovely village of Fairacre for a little over five years. I have enjoyed those years, the children, the school, and the pleasure of running my own schoolhouse and taking part in village life. At last, I believe, I am accepted by the locals, if not as a proper native, at least as "Miss Read up the school", and not as "that new woman pushing herself forward".

Miss Read Good morning, Mrs Pringle. (*To audience*) Mrs Pringle is one of the happy martyrs of this world, hugging her grudges to herself and relishing every insult as a toothsome morsel. Why she carries on the job of school cleaner I can't think. This first day of term is no exception!

Miss Read Did you have a nice holiday?

Mrs Pringle Not much of a holiday for me is it, scrubbing out the whole place, slaving away, trying to set it to rights. I just done that piece of floor you're standing on. (*She stands up painfully, wincing heavily.*) You should set the children a better example Miss Read and watch where you walks and not go round making more work for other folks. You knows my leg is not what it should be, and it's flared up again.

Miss Read Sorry, sorry, Mrs Pringle. Such a lovely sunny day for the first day of term though.

Mrs Pringle Not such a lovely sunny day for those that has to slave away in this place. I can't be everywhere at once. I come up here twice a week regular all through the holidays, and there's not many school cleaners as can say the same. I've worked my fingers to the bone for all these years, as well you knows Miss Read, and for what thanks?

Miss Read Well, I thank you often.

Mrs Pringle But do those dratted children? And that skylight has been up to its old tricks again.

Miss Read Anything in particular?

Mrs Pringle All this 'ere rain has done its worst. Run under the map cupboard, (*Her voice reaches a crescendo*) and nearly got to my stoves!

Miss Read I'll get Mr Willet to have a look.

Mrs Pringle Humph! Bob Willet is all very well, he do know about gardening, and he do help the Vicar a lot as sexton, that I will give him, but he don't understand mechanical things like that dratted skylight. Oh well, I'd better struggle on as best I can and put Miss Clare's classroom to rights. One thing about Miss Clare, she's a proper lady. Knows how to treat people, has a real respect and consideration for other's feelings. Why, her pencil sharpenings are put neat as you like in newspaper, and placed in the wastepaper bin. Not like some I could mention! (*She hobbles off, limping painfully*)

Mr Willet *enters, he is about sixty, the school caretaker.*

Miss Read Good morning, Mr Willet. (*To audience*) Bob Willet is our school caretaker, verger and sexton of Saint Patrick's next door, and general handyman to all Fairacre. He also has the unenviable job of emptying our "*Elsan*" chemical lavatory buckets three times a week.

Mr Willet 'Morning, Miss Read. How's madam sunshine?

*Before **Miss Read** can reply **Miss Clare** enters. She is about sixty, an elegant lady of commanding appearance.*

Miss Clare Good morning, Bob.

Mr Willet Good morning, Dolly.

Miss Clare Miss Read, do you know if Joseph Coggs is to have school dinners?

Miss Read Yes, I believe so.

Miss Clare Well, it may be difficult to get money regularly out of that family – a feckless lot!

Miss Read I'll send a note at home time.

Miss Clare Thank you. That family! I've been teaching Joseph's sister for three years, she's still in the infants' class. There she sits, breathing through her mouth. Still thinks a penny is worth more than a sixpence because it's bigger! What can you expect? Her grandfather never stuck at a job for more than a week and Arthur Coggs took after him. Added to that he married a girl with as much sense as himself, and those children are the result.

Mr Willet You are right about them Coggs! What can you expect with Arthur Coggs as a father?

Miss Read Now, now, Mr Willet.

Mr Willet Well, he's done time in prison, he's a poacher, he's been had up, time and time again for stealing. And he ought to be had up for a lot of other things as well, to my mind.

Miss Read But Mr Willet....

Mr Willet (*Ignoring the interruption*) Why, that bloke hasn't done a decent day's work in years, if ever. All us fools keeps him by giving him the dole and the family allowances. Makes my blood boil!

Miss Clare I am quite worried about Joseph. His mother was taken to hospital last week with some internal trouble connected with the recent baby. The other children are staying with Mrs Coggs' sister, but she has no room for Joseph. He's living in a hand to mouth fashion with his father.

Miss Read Oh dear.

Mr Willet I don't say nothing about Arthur Coggs' drunkenness. Nor don't I say nothing about his hitting of his wife now and again - that's his affair. Nor don't I say nothing about the occasional clip round the ear 'ole for his kids - seeing as kids needs to be brung up respectful - but I do say this. That it's not right to leave that boy alone in that thatched cottage with a candle on, while he spends his evening at the Beetle and Wedge. My Alice and me hears him roaring home nigh on eleven most nights.

Miss Read But the candle would have burnt out by then. Joe would be alone in the dark.

Mr Willet Well, I don't know if that's not a deal safer. Better to be frightened than frizzled. Don't upset yourself, Miss Read, Joe's probably asleep by then.

Miss Read I thought Mrs Waites, next door was looking after him, isn't she Miss Clare? (*To audience*) Miss Clare has taught here for more than forty years. Her home is three miles away in Beech Green. The indomitable lady makes that journey on an ancient bicycle every day. Her knowledge of the local families is as far reaching as invaluable, as on this occasion.

Miss Clare Mrs Waites is well-meaning, but flighty. Never room for more than one thought at a time in her head. Maybe she does take a look at him, maybe not. I have gently questioned Joseph about things, and it seems that when candle does go out, he is too terrified to get out of bed and wets it. When Arthur Coggs eventually gets home, he gives the child a good beating with his belt.

Miss Read This is appalling! I must go and see Mrs Waites at dinner time and see what can be done. I will talk to the Vicar too.

Miss Clare Such a shame, because of all the Coggs' family I have come across, Joseph is by far the brightest. (**Miss Clare** *walks into her classroom, shaking her head sadly*)

Ernest *and* **Anne** *enter holding a cat in an old blanket.*

Ernest It's a stray cat, miss.

Anne It was under Mr Roberts' hedge, Miss.

Ernest It's starving, Miss. (*Sound of cat meowing.*)

Mr Willet (*Examining the bundle*) That's one of Mr Roberts' farm cats. I know it very well. It's like its ma, with one white leg. You take it back boy, or you'll be in trouble.

Ernest *and* **Anne** *look anxiously at* **Miss Read.**

Miss Read You'd better do as Mr Willet says. At playtime you can go back to the place where you found him, and if he's still there you can take down some bread and milk.

Ernest *and* **Anne** *exit with their victim.*

Mr Willet You're too soft with 'em by half. In my day, Mr Brown would have given young Ernest and Anne there a clip round the ear for trying on a trick like that.

Miss Read I don't approve of teachers striking children.

Mr Willet More's the pity. (*He makes for the door; his way is barred by* **Mrs Pringle** *entering bearing a few fragments of a small paint brush on an outstretched hand*)

Mrs Pringle What's all this 'ere, may I ask?

Mr Willet (*Sarcastically*) Don't need much eyesight to see it's been a paint brush in its time.

Mrs Pringle (*Fixing* **Miss Read** *with a stern glance*) Then what's it doing down the plug hole of my wash basin? I scrubbed and scrubbed those wash basins with my very own hands, working my fingers to the bone. Why, you could eat your dinner out of those basins!

Miss Read (*To audience*) Why anyone would want to eat their meal from a wash basin is quite beyond me. (*To* **Mrs Pringle**) Someone's been trying to hide evidence. Put it on my desk and I'll sort it out later. Now I really must ring the bell to start the new term.

Mrs Pringle (*Putting her burden on the desk, stands facing Miss Read, arms akimbo*) What them children need is a bit of old-fashioned discipline.

Mr Willet (*As he and* **Mrs Pringle** *exit together*) I just been telling her that!

Miss Read picks up the school bell and rings it loudly. Sound of children entering the school. **Miss Clare**, **Ernest** and **Anne** return with other children.

Miss Read Good morning children.

Live pupils and recorded voices together Good morning, Miss Read.

Miss Clare Good morning children.

Live pupils and recorded voices together Good morning, Miss Clare.

Miss Read We will stand to sing "*All Things Bright and Beautiful*".

All those on-stage sing, together with recorded voices and the audience. Lights fade, **Miss Clare** *returns to her classroom.*

Miss Read (*To* **Ernest** *and* **Anne** *who are sitting behind the audience*) Jimmy, what happened with the cat?

Anne Mr Roberts was up the yard, and we told him about the poor old stray, and he said it wasn't no stray, but one of his'n.

Miss Read His.

Anne That's right, miss, his'n.

Ernest So we just come back.

Miss Read Came back.

Ernest Like I said. (*Miss Read lets out a sigh and gives up*)

Miss Read Take out your pencils and paper for a test. (*Groans from the pupils*) First question. If a man had twelve chickens…

The Reverend Gerald Partridge *enters, he is vague in his manner.*

Rev Partridge I'm sorry to interrupt, but I was just passing and thought I would have a word with you.

Miss Read Of course. (*To the class*) Turn over your test papers and write out the twelve times table. (*Groans from the pupils*) How can I help you Vicar? (*To audience*) The Reverend Gerald Partridge has been vicar of Fairacre and adjoining parishes for only four years, and so is looked upon as a foreigner by most of his parishioners. He is intellectual, extremely well-read and loves all his parishioners with a full heart, seeing only goodness in them all.

Rev Partridge I wonder, could you look at this list of hymns and teach the children them this year? (*He hands Miss Read the list*)

Miss Read (*Scanning the list*) Yes, but I don't think this Milton poem set as a hymn *"and speckled vanity will sicken soon and die, and leprous sin will melt from earthly mould"* is at all suitable. Quite beyond the comprehension of young children.

Rev Partridge Very well, my dear, very well. Just as you think best. Let us leave that hymn until they are older. I also wondered my dear Miss Read, if you had heard anything about the school closing? Anything from the office?

Miss Read No, only rumours. They fly around so often; I don't let them bother me unduly.

Rev Partridge I wanted you to know that I have had no official message about such a possibility. I pray that I may never have one, but should it be so, please rest assured that I should let you know at once.

Miss Read Thank you. I know you would.

Rev Partridge Quite, quite. Well, I must be off. Mrs Partridge asked me to pick up something at the Post Office, but for the life of me I can't remember what it is. I wonder if I should go back and ask?

Miss Read No doubt Mrs Lamb will know and have it waiting for you.

Rev Partridge I'm sure you're right. I will call there first. No point in worrying my wife unnecessarily. How astute you are Miss Read!

Linda *rushes in.*

Linda Miss, one of them from the babies class has been to the lavatory on the lobby floor.

Miss Read That is what is known as a contradiction of terms, but I'll come at once.

Rev Partridge In that case I must let you return to your duties. (*He hastens away*)

Fade lights/music. **Miss Read** *cleans the blackboard and leaves.*

Scene Two

The following Saturday Morning. The School House. **Miss Read** *is sitting at her table, a pot of coffee and some biscuits on a plate next to her.* **Mrs Pringle** *appears with her black oil-cloth bag which accompanies her everywhere.*

Mrs Pringle I brung you a fresh cabbage. I know you likes to cook at the weekend. A fresh bit of veg is much better than that stale old stuff the village shop sells.(*She hands over a cabbage*)

Miss Read Thank you Mrs Pringle. Have a cup of coffee with me.

Mrs Pringle (*Graciously*) I don't mind if I do.

Miss Read (*To herself*) And I don't mind if you don't!

Mrs Pringle Pardon?

Miss Read Nothing, nothing! Do sit down Mrs Pringle, I will fetch another cup. (*She exits.*)

Mrs Pringle (*Sitting heavily on the chair calling to* **Miss Read**.) I see'd you've got plenty of bindweed in your border, and twitch. No need to have twitch if you weeds regular. (**Miss Read** *returns, sits and pours* **Mrs Pringle** *her coffee.*)

Miss Read Have a biscuit.

Mrs Pringle (*Takes a chocolate biscuit.*) I used to be very partial to these chocolate biscuits until they doubled in price pretty nearly. Now I buys Osborne. Just as nourishing, and don't fatten you so much. At least, so Dr Martin said when he gave me my diet sheet.

Miss Read A diet sheet?

Mrs Pringle Yes, I'm to lose three stone. No starch, no sugar, no fat, and no alcohol - though the last's no hardship, considering I signed the pledge as a child.

Miss Read Then should you be eating that biscuit, and drinking coffee with cream in it?

Mrs Pringle I'm starting tomorrow. (*She takes a swift bite at the biscuit.*) I said to Doctor Martin. It's all very well but I needs my nourishment, slaving away at that school, day in, day out. But, there again, maybe I won't have to carry on giving my all to Fairacre school.

Miss Read Why not, Mrs Pringle, not thinking of giving it up are you?

Mrs Pringle You've heard about our school shutting, I suppose?

Miss Read Oh, that rumour again? Where did you hear that old tale?

Mrs Pringle Maybe an old tale to you. Pringle said there was a lot of talk about it in The Beetle last night.

Miss Read I wouldn't believe everything you are told, Mrs Pringle, especially if it comes from The Beetle and Wedge!

Mrs Pringle But, the whole village is talking about it! Everybody knows what's going on it seems. Except you.

Miss Read (*Attempts to speak but is swept aside by* **Mrs Pringle** *in full spate*)

Mrs Pringle It's not only Fairacre neither, but my cousin at Beech Green says they're going to build on to Mr Annett's school and send our lot over there in a bus. Won't suit some of 'em. Some seems to think the infants will stay here, but as I said to Florrie - that's my cousin at Beech Green - and a flighty one she used to be as a girl, but has steadied down wonderful now she's got eight children - I said to her, as straight as I'm saying to you now, Miss Read, what call would the office have to keep open all that great school for a handful of fives to sevens? Don't make sense, I said, and I repeat it now to you Miss Read. It just don't make no sense.

Miss Read No indeed.

Mrs Pringle Take the heating, sacks of good coke them stoves need during the winter, not to mention blacklead and brushes and a cinder pail. They all takes us taxpayers' money. Then there's brooms and dusters, and bar soap and floor cloths, which cost a small fortune.

Miss Read And all the books, paper, and pencils of course.

Mrs Pringle (*Doubtfully*) Well, yes. I suppose they needs all that stuff. But it stands to reason that it's cheaper for all the whole boiling lot to go on a bus to Beech Green, though what the petrol costs these days to trundle them back and forth, I shudders to think.

Miss Read Well it may not happen yet, we've had these scaremongering tales before.

Mrs Pringle Maybe. But this time I've heard it from a good many folks, and when have our numbers at Fairacre School ever been so low? I don't like it, Miss Read. I feels in my bones a preposition. My mother, God rest her, had second sight, and sometimes I thinks I takes after her. (*She rises majestically.*) You wants to get rid of that bindweed, before it takes over. (**Mrs Pringle** *exits without a trace of a limp*)

Miss Read That woman always has the last word! Let's hope her "preposition" is wrong.

Fade lights. Music.

Miss Read *returns to the classroom. and writes the new date on the blackboard. Thursday 6^(th) October 1955.*

Scene Three

Miss Read *Stands in front of her class. She is leading them through a song.*

Pupils (*Clapping*) One man went to mow, went to mow a meadow...

Miss Pitt *enters the classroom. She is wearing a fawn hat, fawn overcoat, even her complexion is fawn. She looks around the room in distaste. The children shudder to a halt.*

Miss Pitt I am Miss Pitt, the new needlework inspector.

Miss Read Nice to meet you. (*She extends her hand;* **Miss Pitt** *ignores it*) Children, take out your reading books, and read quietly.

Miss Pitt This doesn't appear to be a very convenient time to call.

Miss Read It is no bother to show you our work. (*She takes the girls' sewing from the desk drawer*) The bigger girls are making aprons with cross-over straps. That brings in buttonholes. The small girls are making bibs or hankies. (*She shows* **Miss Pitt** *a couple of examples*)

Miss Pitt Oh dear! Oh dear! I'm afraid this is very out-of-date.

Miss Read Out-of-date? But children can always do with pinafores!

Miss Pitt (*As though addressing a very backward child*) We just don't, we just don't expect young children like this to do such fine work. Pure Victoriana, this! All this hemming and oversewing, and buttonholing - it just isn't done these days. Plenty of thick bright wool, crewel needles, not too small, and coarse crash, or better still, hessian to work on, and the very simplest of stitches. And as for these poor babies with their hankies. (*She gives a high affected laugh*) Canvas mats, or a simple pochette is the sort of thing they should be attempting. Eyestrain, you know!

Miss Read But none of them wear glasses, and they've always been perfectly happy making these things for themselves or their families. And surely, they should learn the elementary stitches?

Miss Pitt No, I'm not criticizing, it's all a matter of approach. Have you any hessian in the school?

Miss Read Only a very small amount for the babies. I've used up all our money on this cotton material. I'm afraid the aprons and so on will have to go forward.

Miss Pitt A pity. Ah well! I will call in again sometime next term and see if I can give you some more help. We do want to bring colour and life into these rather drab surroundings, don't we? One meets such hardworking people in this job, such really worthy fellow-creatures. It's a great privilege to be able to guide them, I find. Goodbye, Miss Annett. This is Beech Green School, isn't it?

Miss Read This is Fairacre School. I am Miss Read. Mr Annett is headmaster at Beech Green School.

Miss Pitt Then he is next on my list. (*They make for the door*)

Miss Read Turn right along the lane, and it's about two or three miles along the Caxley road.

Miss Pitt Good afternoon, Miss Read.

Miss Read Good afternoon, Miss Pitt. (**Miss Pitt** *exits*)

Miss Read (*To audience*) And what Mr Annett will have to say to that fawn fiend I should dearly love to know!

Now children, we will get ready to go across to the Church to help decorate for harvest.

Linda *comes to* **Miss Read's** *desk.*

Linda Miss Read, Miss Clare's been and fallen over!

Fade lights/music.

Scene Four

The school house half an hour later.

(**Dr Martin** *is drying his hands on a clean tea-towel, whistling tunelessly to himself.* **Miss Read** *enters*)

Miss Read How is she? (*To audience*) Dr Martin has been the G.P. in Fairacre and surrounding villages for a very long time. He knows the histories of the village families intimately.

Dr Martin She'll be all right now; but I'd like her to stay here for the night if you can have her.

Miss Read Of course.

Dr Martin She's resting in your sitting room.

Miss Read I see. Has she needed to call you in before? She's said nothing to me about these attacks.

Dr Martin Had them on and off for two years now, the silly girl.

Miss Read Oh dear.

Dr Martin She will have to give this up, you know. Should have done so last year, but she's as obstinate as her father was. Do your best to make her see it. I'll call in tomorrow morning. (*He puts his head round the door of the sitting room*) Now Dolly, stay there and rest. You'll do my dear. You'll do!

Miss Read Thank you very much, Dr Martin.

Dr Martin Not at all Miss Read, cheerio. (*He exits, whistling*)

Miss Read Goodbye. (*Sound of ancient car driving off*)

The front door knocker sounds. (**Miss Read** *exits. Voices off stage.* **Miss Read** (*Resignedly*) Mrs Pringle, do come in.

Miss Read *and* **Mrs Pringle** *enter.* **Mrs Pringle** *is limping heavily.*

Mrs Pringle I won't be able to clear up very much in that dratted school this afternoon. My poor leg has flared up again! (*She winces heavily*)

Miss Read How unfortunate.

Mrs Pringle More than unfortunate for me what has to bear the pain. But as my mother used to say - you're a giver, Maud my girl, a true giver to others. And, as for them stoves, I doubt my leg will stand dragging up the village street tomorrow morning to light them.

Miss Read Don't bother! I shall have the whole school in my classroom, and in any case, we shall spend quite a time over at the church.

Mrs Pringle Sad about Miss Clare. A fit, so I gather.

Miss Read No, not a fit.

Mrs Pringle Can't hardly ever do nothing about fits. My sister's boy, why, he's had 'em since he were a dot. Just after whooping-cough it started; my sister had a terrible time with him over whooping-cough. Tried everything! Dr Martin's stuff never helped - all that did was to take the varnish off the mantlepiece where the bottle stood; and Alice Willet's old mother - who was a wise old party though she lost her hair terrible towards the end - she recommended a fried mouse, eaten whole to stop the cough.

Miss Read Surely not.

Mrs Pringle Ain't you never heard of that? A good old-fashioned cure that is. Never done Percy much good. These 'ere fits come on after that. Same as poor Miss Clare. It's the swallowing of the tongue that makes it more trying like.

Miss Read I'm sure it is, although as I told you, Miss Clare has not had a fit.

Mrs Pringle Well I can't stand here gossiping with you all afternoon, harvest supper tonight.

Miss Read Yes, cheese and salad, thanks to Mrs Partridge and Mrs Willet.

Mrs Pringle I knows that. Methodists had cottage pie at their harvest!

Miss Read I'll see you out, Mrs Pringle.

Miss Read *leads out to the front door.* **Mrs Pringle** *trots behind without a sign of a limp.*

Miss Clare *enters looking pale and frail* **Miss Read** *returns.*

Miss Clare I heard. (**Miss Read** *can say nothing*)

Miss Clare I heard what Dr Martin said. He's right, you know. I shall go as soon as possible. (*Silence in the room*) Or do you think I should go at once? Is that what you think? Do you wish I'd gone before? You must have noticed that I was not doing my job as I should.

Miss Read I don't think that at all. Don't think about plans this evening. We'll see what Dr Martin says tomorrow and talk it over then.

Miss Clare Should you telephone the office, do you think dear? It closes at five, you know, and if you need a supply teacher?

Miss Read I shall manage easily tomorrow on my own, we shall go over to the church to get it ready for harvest festival. I can ring the office when you've seen Dr Martin. Don't worry about a thing. (*She moves to* **Miss Clare** *and gently puts her arm around her*)

Miss Clare *faces front, tears flowing down her cheeks.*

Miss Clare I always loved harvest festival.

Music "We Plough the Fields and Scatter,"

Lights fade.

Scene Five

The school room, the following morning. The blackboard states Friday 7th October 1955.

Miss Read *stands in front of the class.*

Miss Read Now children, I would like you to write a poem about Autumn.

Ernest What - rhyming and that?

Miss Read Yes, rhyming.

Linda How many verses, Miss Read?

Miss Read As many as you can think of.

Anne Do us have to make it go thumpity-thumpity like that "Half a league, half a league" bit you read us? *(General chattering and sighing from the children.)*

Miss Read Yes, of course rhythm is expected. Now, come along, stop chattering and start working. *(The pupils start working, the room is silent.* **The Rev Partridge** *enters)*

Rev Partridge My dear Miss Read, so sorry to interrupt your work. Good afternoon, children.

The Pupils *(Standing.)* Good afternoon, Reverend Partridge.

Miss Read Now, sit down and carry on with writing your poems. How can I help you Vicar?

Rev Partridge It's about the poor Coggs family. I gather Mrs Waites was able to help with poor Joseph.

Miss Read Yes, she was. Very sensible and helpful. She let Joseph share Jimmy's bedroom. But of course, Mrs Coggs is back home now.

Rev Partridge Indeed, Miss Read. Are things any better in the household?

Miss Read Money as always is a big problem. I think Mrs Coggs is just about managing. All rather poverty stricken, I'm sorry to say.

Rev Partridge Well, I would be happy to help financially if I could without causing embarrassment to dear Mrs Coggs. She has quite enough to worry about as it is. Sometimes, Miss Read, I do wonder if we will ever achieve Lloyd George's pledge of making Britain a fit country for heroes to live in.

Miss Read Try not to worry about it. I know that Mrs Moffat and some of the other mothers hand on clothes when their own children grow out of them. Of course, the whole Coggs family would be better off without Arthur, lazy great bully that he is!

Rev Partridge Harsh words, Miss Read, harsh words! He is one of my flock, you know, even if he has wandered somewhat astray. Now, about the managers' meeting next week. I'm in rather a quandary. My dear wife has inadvertently invited all the sewing ladies, so the dining-room will be in use. The table, you know, so convenient for cutting out. And the drawing-room is being decorated, and everything is under shrouds - no, not shrouds-furniture covers - no, loose covers - no, I don't think that is the correct term either.

Miss Read Dust sheets.

Rev Partridge Yes, indeed! What a grasp you have of everything, dear Miss Read, no wonder the children do so well! Yes, well, you see my difficulty. And my study is so small, and very untidy, I fear. I suppose we could manage something in the hall, but it is rather draughty, and the painters are in and out, you know, about their work, and like to have their little wireless going with music.

Miss Read Don't worry, we could meet here.

Rev Partridge That would be quite perfect. Thank you Miss Read. I shall make a note in my diary at once. By the way, no more news about the possible closing. Have you heard anything?

Miss Read Only from Mrs Pringle. Nothing official.

Rev Partridge Ah well, no news is good news, they say. We'll hear more perhaps at our managers' meeting. I gather that nice Mr Canterbury, who is in charge of the Caxley Office, is coming out himself. (**Miss Read** *looks concerned*) No, I don't mean Canterbury, do I? Now, what is that fellow's name? I know it's a cathedral city. Winchester? Rochester? Dear, oh dear, I shall forget my own soon.

Miss Read Salisbury.

Rev Partridge Thank you I shall make a careful note of his name. I shouldn't like to upset such an important fellow. (*He vanishes into the lobby*)

Miss Read (*To audience*) I think it far more likely that the important fellow will upset us!

Music

Scene Six

The blackboard states, Monday 10th October 1955. The following afternoon in the school. **Miss Read, Miss Clare, Rev Partridge, Mrs Pringle, Mr Willet, Mr Roberts,** *and the* **pupils** *are gathered.*

Rev Partridge……. And so, after many years of loyal service to Fairacre School, indeed more than forty years of dedicated service, it is time to say goodbye to dear Miss Clare. Miss Clare, I will remind you, joined this school as a monitress at the age of thirteen and has remained at her post except for a very short break when she nursed her mother through her final illness some years ago. Miss Clare has meant a lot to all of us gathered here this afternoon, and indeed to generations of young children who have been in her care. It is impossible to repay all those years of selfless devotion to this school and the pupils, but we would like you, dear Miss Clare, to have a small token of our affection and gratitude. (*He hands* **Miss Clare** *an envelope.* **Linda** *appears with a bunch of garden flowers and presents them to* **Miss Clare** *and curtsies. The assembled people all clap*)

Miss Clare Thank you all. Reverend Partridge, for those very kind words. Thank you to the School Managers for your very kind gifts. Thank you lastly to the very kind children of Fairacre School for the lovely flowers.

The clapping re-commences. The cast members leave. **Miss Read, Rev Partridge, Mr Willet** *and* **Mr Roberts remain.**

Mr Roberts Now, these rumours about our school closing.

Miss Read (To audience) Mr Roberts is the local farmer and a very practical school manager.

Rev Partridge Indeed, Roberts. As I informed Miss Read, Mr Oxford, from the Caxley office is coming to our managers' meeting next week.

Miss Read Mr Salisbury.

Rev Partridge Quite so, Miss Read, Mr Salisbury.

Mr Roberts We've got to be firm about this. Say no from the outset. I mean, what's village life coming to?

Miss Read How do you mean?

Mr Roberts Well, we used to have a village bobby. Remember Trumper, padre?

Rev Partridge Yes, I do remember Trumper, he was a splendid fellow.

Mr Willet Exactly. Used to hear old Trumper puffin' round the village every night about two o'clock making sure everything was in order.

Mr Roberts So sensible. We need more police. That's half the trouble these days.

Mr Willet And what's more, he gave any young scallywag a good clip round the ear'ole, on the spot, and stopped a peck of wrongdoing. What happens now? Some ruddy Juvenile Court months and months later when the kid's forgotten all about it.

Rev Partridge Quite. But we were discussing the possibility of the school closure.

Mr Roberts It's the same principle. You need direct contact - that's the unique quality of village life. We lost the village bobby, that was a link broken. Far worse to lose our village school.

Rev Partridge Yes, too little spread too thinly.

Mr Willet Same as having to share you Vicar, with Beech Green and Springbourne. Why, I remember before your day, of course, when the Vicar was just for Fairacre, and you could reckon to see him any time you wanted, if you was in trouble. He'd be in his study or the garden, or in church or visiting in the parish. Now he can be anywhere.

Rev Partridge (*Sadly*) Yes, indeed Willet.

Mr Willet Not that it can be altered, and a very good job you do, but it's not the same.

Rev Partridge Thank you Willet. We need to discuss this with Mr Ely when we see him next week.

Miss Read Mr Salisbury.

Rev Partridge Mr Salisbury. I suppose there's no hope of keeping this school open for infants only? I imagine the biggest objection would be the idea of sending our infants on a bus to Beech Green.

Miss Read It's too small as it is. Even if the Beech Green infants were brought here, I expect the authority would say both schools would be too small.

Mr Roberts The trouble is people are moving away from the village. Dave Stevens is thinking about moving to Caxley.

Mr Willet A pity, such a good herdsman.

Mr Roberts He is. Took ten years to learn his skills. Be lucky to get another chap to replace him.

Miss Read And his two children leaving the school.

Mr Roberts I know, what can I do? He'll get double the wages I can afford to pay. I know he gets the farm cottage rent free, kept in good order too, even if I say so myself. He's been offered a council house in Caxley, paying half his wages in rent, and spending his days pressing some buttons in a factory in Caxley! What a waste.

Rev Partridge We must talk about our village school.

Mr Roberts If we give in, even before we start, we're betraying the village as I see it. Our Fairacre children get a jolly sound grounding. You've only got to look at the percentage we get through the eleven-plus to go to the Caxley grammar schools. I am firmly against the idea of closure. We need to nip this in the bud.

There is general agreement among the others.

Mr Willet Don't you worry Miss Read. Us'll rout anybody who tries to close our school. (*He marches out*)

Mr Roberts We will indeed! (*He follows* **Mr Willet**)

Rev Partridge Never fear, dear Miss Read, Fairacre school will be here for another hundred years.

Miss Read I hope so.

Scene Seven

The following morning in the school house. **Miss Read** *is sipping a cup of tea.* **Mrs Pringle** *appears.* **Miss Read** *stands to greet her.*

Miss Read Good morning, Mrs Pringle.

Mrs Pringle Mornin' Miss Read. I'm in trouble!

Miss Read Oh dear, what's the matter?

Mrs Pringle It's that dratted Minnie. Pringle's niece.

Miss Read Oh no! What's happened?

Mrs Pringle You may well ask! She's at my place. I left her grizzling in the kitchen, and the children are in the garden. I've dared them to put a single foot on the flower beds, unless they wants to be skinned alive. I can't say fairer than that to them.

Miss Read Sit down, Mrs Pringle, and have a cup of tea.

Mrs Pringle Thank you, Miss Read, I don't mind if I do.

(**Miss Read** *pours a cup of tea and passes to* **Mrs Pringle**)

Mrs Pringle That man, her Ern, has up and left our Minnie. What's more, he's left his children, and hers and that one of theirs, to look after, while he gallivants with that woman who's no better than she should be.

Miss Read Perhaps he'll come back.

Mrs Pringle Not him! He's gone for good. And do you know who he's run off with?

Miss Read No.

Mrs Pringle You'll never guess. That Mrs Fowler from Tyler's Row. Next to them Coggses.

Miss Read Mrs Fowler! I can't imagine anyone falling for her! She's absolutely without any charms at all!

Mrs Pringle The scheming hussy! It's my belief she knew he had an insurance policy coming out this month. Well, it wouldn't be for his looks, would it?

Miss Read I agree. But you never know.

Mrs Pringle But, the top and the bottom of it is - how's Minnie going to live? Oh, I expect she'll get the National Security and Family Allowance, and all that, but she'll need a bit of work as well, I reckons, if she's to keep that council house on in Springbourne.

Miss Read Won't he provide some money?

Mrs Pringle That'll be the day, unless Minnie takes him to court, and who's got the time and money to bother with all that?

Miss Read (*Reluctantly*) If she really needs work, I could give her half a day here cleaning windows, and silver, and things.

Mrs Pringle That's a very kind thought, Miss Read. Of course, he had the cheek, with that woman, to take the furniture from our Minnie's place too.

Miss Read But, can he? Isn't it the marital home or whatever they call it?

Mrs Pringle Whether he can or he can't, he done it. And that Mrs Fowler, she was at the bottom of it. It was that cat as put him up to it. And her nephew had his van waiting by Minnie's gate to put all the stuff in. All planned and plotted, you see. And off they drove, leaving our Minnie without a frying pan in the house.

Miss Read Nothing at all?

Mrs Pringle (*Tutting with impatience*) No, no, they never took the lot, I'll give 'em that. But they took two armchairs, and the kitchen table, and no end of china, and the upstairs curtains, and some cooking pots, and the frying pan. So of course, Minnie and them dratted children haven't had no dinner. So, it looks to me, Miss Read, as Minnie will be very glad to take up your offer of some work here. She's got all that stuff to buy anew, and money's very tight anyway. I'll tell her to come up and see you to arrange things.

Miss Read (*Faintly*) Thank you, Mrs Pringle.

Mrs Pringle That's all right. (*Heaving herself to her feet*) Well. I'd better hurry back and see what damage those little varmints of Minnie's have done. When shall I tell her to come?

Miss Read She'd better come one evening. There's no hurry tell her. And if she gets a post elsewhere, I shall quite understand.

Mrs Pringle Right! I'll let her know. But I wouldn't trust her with glass, if I was you, or any good china. She's a bit clumsy that way. Sometimes I wonder if our Minnie is right in the head!

Mrs Pringle *limps off, dragging her leg. She encounters* **Mr Willet**.

Mrs Pringle Morning, Bob Willet.

Mr Willet Morning Maud.

Miss Read (*To audience*) Minnie Pringle's I.Q is extremely low. She is very scatterbrained as well. Looks like I've saddled myself with her.

Mr Willet Morning, Miss Read.

Miss Read Good morning, Mr Willet. Would you like a cup of tea?

Mr Willet No thanks , Miss Read. I just come over to tell you I been tryin' to sort them windows out over school.

Miss Read Thank you.

Mr Willet They's stuck with the damp. Needs to be planed really, but then, come the summer you'd get a proper draught. Bad as that blasted skylight. Useless to waste time and money on it. Been like it since I sat in that classroom as a boy; be the same when I'm dead and gone, I shouldn't wonder.

Miss Read You're down in the dumps today, not like you.

Mr Willet Had some bad news. My brother's gone home.

Miss Read Oh, I'm sorry.

Mr Willet Well, he'd been bad for some time, but you know how it is, you don't ever think of anyone younger than you going home, do you?

Miss Read It's a horrible shock.

Mr Willet Sid was the youngest. He was quite a scholar. Used to sit in the back row over school when old Mr John Brown was headmaster. He could have gone to the grammar school, but with all five of us to keep, Dad said he'd best get out working. Sid never complained and he made a durn fine cabinet maker in the end, but I reckons he minded a bit about not going to Caxley Grammar School.

Miss Read It seems unfair.

Mr Willet It's a funny thing, when someone dies, you never remember them as they were then, but always as children. I saw Sid last week. But all I can see now is Sid about ten, lugging the rush basket with our school dinners up the hill here to Fairacre school. Or swinging our sister Molly round by her hands or feeding his pet rabbit.

Miss Read Perhaps that's as it should be.

Mr Willet (*Looking into the distance*) That's the third death this year. Like a stab wound, every time. Leaves a hole, and a little of your life-blood drains away. (**Miss Read** *is too moved to comment*) Well, this won't do. Life's got to go on, ain't it? (**Mr Willet** *stumps off to meet it*)

Scene Eight

The Schoolroom the following week. The blackboard states Monday 17th October. There is a gentle chatter of the school pupils in the background.

Ernest (*Tearfully*) I been an' lost me dinner money Miss. It was in my pocket, Miss. All scrunched up it were, with these 'ere. (*He takes out of his pocket four marbles, a stub of pencil, a lump of bubble gum, and a jagged piece of red glass*)

Miss Read You'll cut yourself on that. Put it into the wastepaper basket.

Ernest But it's off of my brother's rear lamp.

Miss Read Well, put it, and all the other rubbish on my desk until home time. (**Ernest** *does so*) Now think Ernest. Did you take the ten shilling note out of your pocket on the way to school?

Linda Yes, he did Miss. He showed it to me Miss. Said he betted I didn't have as much money.

Anne That's right Miss. And it was windy. Blowing about like a flag it were. I bet it's blowed over the hedge.

Linda And some old cow's eaten it.

Anne Or some old tramp's picked it up.

Linda Or some old bird's got it in its nest. (**Ernest** *starts to cry*)

Miss Read You must go back over your tracks, Ernest, and search, and someone had better go with you. Two pairs of eyes are better than one. (*Silence falls in the classroom*)

Miss Read Linda. (**Ernest** *and* **Linda** *exit*)

Miss Read We will say the seven times table together.

Miss Read and Pupils One 7 is 7. Two 7s are 14….. (*The pupils get more uncertain as the table progresses*) **Ernest** *and* **Linda** *enter.*

Ernest We found it, miss.

Linda Guess where?

Miss Read In the hedge?

Ernest No.

Anne In the duckpond?

Linda No.

Miss Read In your pocket after all?

Ernest No.

Anne In the playground?

Linda No.

Miss Read That's enough. Tell us where.

Ernest In a cow pat, just by the school gate. So stuck up it was, it couldn't blow away. Weren't that lucky?

Miss Read Wipe it with a damp cloth in the lobby and bring it back. Don't let go of it for one second. Understand? While we're about it, we'll have an early playtime, I think.

Anne Good, I hates seven times table.

Miss Read That will come later!

The children surge out noisily to play. **Ernest** *lingers.*

Ernest I see'd a policeman coming out of Joe Coggs' place Miss.

Miss Read Never mind. Mr and Mrs Coggs will deal with it I expect. Off you go Ernest, out to play with the others. (**Ernest** *exits.* **Mrs Pringle** *enters with a black oil cloth bag from which she takes out some clean teacloths*)

Mrs Pringle Just brung up these cloths.

Miss Read Thank you. Couldn't you bring them up later when you come to wash the dinner plates?

Mrs Pringle No. I 'as to wait for the oil man then. Them tapers he sold me last week are no use at all! Heard about Arthur Coggs?

Mr Willet *enters wielding a large broom.*

Mr Willet Thought I'd better sort out that dratted coke pile after play time. Heard about Arthur Coggs?

Miss Read Joe was a little late this morning, he told me a policeman was at their house.

Mrs Pringle That's right. "Making enquiries", they are!

Mr Willet That's what I heard too. About lead being pinched from Mr Mawne's summer house, here in Fairacre! A mort of other crimes too, I'll wager!

Miss Read Oh no.

Mr Willet Oh yes. What's to stop them blighters pinchin' the new lead off of the church roof? Cost a mort of money to put on. It'd make a fine haul for some of these robbers.

Mrs Pringle They wouldn't dare take the Lord's property. Not Saint Patrick's.

Miss Read I don't think they care much whose property it is. It's just how easily they can turn it into hard cash.

Mrs Pringle My sister in Caxley told me the most shocking thing happened all up the road next to hers.

Mr Willet What?

Mrs Pringle *looks round the classroom, then speaks in a low and conspiratorial voice. The three heads all bend together.*

Mrs Pringle Well, these lead thieves came one night and went along all the outside lavatories and cut out every bit of piping from the cistern to the pan!

Mr Willet No!

Mrs Pringle They did. True as I'm standing here.

Mr Willet Every house?

Mrs Pringle Not quite all. Mr Jarvis, him what was once usher at the court, happened to be in his when they reached it, so they cleared off pretty smartish.

Miss Read Did they catch them?

Mrs Pringle Not one of 'em. Still at large, they are. I bet that are the same lot what took Mr Mawne's lead off his summer house. Including that Arthur Coggs.

Miss Read Now, Mrs Pringle, we know nothing about Arthur Coggs being connected with lead stealing.

Mrs Pringle I do!

Miss Read But, you can't just pin everything that's crooked on Arthur Coggs.

Mrs Pringle Why not? More times than not, you'd be right.

Miss Read We don't know that he's guilty yet.

Mr Willet I do. That Arthur Coggs. He makes my blood boil, great useless article. Why the Almighty saw fit to put wasps, adders and Arthur Coggs into this world, is beyond me. Cheerio, Miss Read. (*He and* **Mrs Pringle** *stump off.*)

Scene Nine

The schoolhouse later that day. **Miss Read** *is marking books. She sees*

Minnie Pringle, *an untidily dressed, scatterbrained woman, arriving.*

Miss Read Hello, Minnie, come in.

Minnie Auntie says you could do with some help.

Miss Read (*Reluctantly*) Well yes, would two hours a week suit you?

Minnie (*Scratching her tousled locks with a silver-varnished nail*) Same pay as auntie?

Miss Read Yes.

Minnie O.K. What wants doin'?

Miss Read We'll discuss that in a minute. When can you come? I gather you have some work already.

Minne You can say that again. I goes to Mrs Partridge Mondays, Vicar fixed that up for me. Then I goes to Mrs Mawne on Wednesday mornings, but that's all scrubbin'. Mr Mawne don't want no one to touch his butterfly drawers, and stuffed birds and that, though I offered to give 'em a good dusting. He's a funny chap aint 'e? Then Thursday evenings I does out the hall 'cos auntie says it's getting too much for her, and the committee gentleman said it was all right for me to do it. Though I don't know if I shall stick it long.

Miss Read Why not?

Minnie Mucky. Bits of sausage roll, and jam tarts squashed between the floorboards, and the sink gets stopped with tea leaves.

Miss Read Don't they use tea bags?

Minnie Cor! You're a marvel! I'll tell 'em you said that! It's the cricket tea ladies as does it, I reckons. Though them Scouts and Cubs isn't above mucking things up in spite of all them oaths they take. Then there's that la-di-da drama club.

Miss Read The Fairacre Players, yes.

Minnie They thinks they own the village hall that lot. Auntie says they're show-offs, all of them.

Miss Read They put good productions on.

Minnie When they remembers their lines! Tea bags is the answer, of course it is. I'll tell 'em you suggested that.

Miss Read I'm glad to be of help. (*To audience*) I very likely will be ostracised by all who use the village hall! (*To Minnie*) Is that all the work you do?

Minnie (*Truculently*) I has to keep my own place tidy at Springbourne.

Miss Read Of course, of course. I meant any more work in Fairacre.

Minnie I likes to keep Saturday free.

Miss Read Naturally. I shouldn't want you to give up your weekends. What about Friday afternoons?

Minnie I shops on Fridays.

Miss Read Wednesday then?

Minnie Auntie comes up here Wednesdays.

Miss Read Of course. Tuesday any good?

Minnie I goes to Springbourne Tuesdays, 'cos it's double Green Shield stamps day at the shop.

Miss Read What's wrong with Monday?

Minnie The Vicar.

Miss Read Well, Minnie, when can you come?

Minnie Friday afternoons.

Miss Read (*Taking a deep breath*) But I thought you said you went shopping on Friday.

Minnie Not till six o'clock. It's late night Caxley.

Miss Read Very well then, let's say from two until four on Friday afternoon. Or one-thirty to three-thirty if that suits you better.

Minnie Is that har'past one?

Miss Read (*Faintly*) Yes.

Minnie (*Scratching her hair again*) Well, that's fine and dandy. I'll come at har'past one and do two hours, and go at - what time did you say?

Miss Read Half-past three. I shall be back from school after that.

Minnie What about me money then?

Miss Read I shall leave it on the mantlepiece, just as I do for Mrs Pringle. Now, when you come this week, I should like you to clean the upstairs windows please. The dusters and window cleaning liquid are both in the cupboard under the kitchen sink. Can you manage that?

Minnie I spec' so. Ain't you got no meths and newspapers? It does a treat. Keeps the flies off too.

Miss Read No Minnie, I dislike the smell of methylated spirits.

Minnie My uncle drinks it. Gets real high on it. They picks him up regular in Caxley, and it's only on meths.

Miss Read Now Minnie, I must get to the managers' meeting at the school.

Minnie They're gonna close Fairacre school ain't they, same as Springbourne?

Miss Read I very much hope not.

Minnie O.K. See you Friday, if not before. (*She totters off*)

Scene Ten

The School Classroom. The blackboard states Thursday 20th October 1955.

Rev Partridge, Mr Roberts, Mrs Lamb, Miss Quinn, *and* **Mr Salisbury** *are there.* **Miss Read** *enters and takes her seat.*

Rev Partridge Good evening, everybody and welcome to our meeting of the Fairacre school managers. This is Mr Salisbury from Caxley Education Office. Fairacre school managers, Mr Salisbury. Miss Quinn, Mrs Lamb, Mr Roberts and Miss Read whom of course you know. (*They all nod and shake hands with Mr Salisbury*) I wonder, Mr Salisbury have you any particular message from the office? We have been hearing some rather disturbing rumours.

Mr Salisbury Oh! What about?

Mr Roberts (*Bluntly*) Might close the school.

Miss Quinn Really? I hadn't heard a thing.

Mrs Lamb Well, Miss Quinn, you must be the only person in Fairacre who has not heard anything. Lots of folk ask me about it when they come to the Post Office.

Rev Partridge Quite, quite. Now, dear ladies and gentlemen, may we hear what Mr Exeter has to say, please?

Mr Salisbury (*Taking his new name in his stride*) Well, I don't know just what you have been hearing in Fairacre, but I can assure you that the office would always consult with the managers of any school as soon as the possibility of closure cropped up.

Mr Roberts And has it?

Mr Salisbury (*Cautiously*) There is always a chance of really small schools becoming uneconomic.

Mrs Lamb Fairacre's not really small.

Miss Quinn I like small schools anyway.

Mr Roberts Much more friendly.

Mr Salisbury There are certain disadvantages. Lack of team games, for instance. No specialist teachers on the staff for certain subjects. Children can get deprived.

Mrs Lamb Deprived? Our children aren't deprived are they, Miss Read?

Miss Read I hope not.

Mr Roberts But what about Fairacre? Are you sharpening the knife for us?

Mr Salisbury Nothing will be done without your knowledge and co-operation.

Miss Read But it's on the cards? Is that it?

Mr Salisbury Numbers are going down steadily. We must assess each case on its merit. Certainly, Fairacre is costing us a lot of money to maintain, and the children might well be better off at a larger school.

Miss Read Such as Beech Green.

Mr Salisbury (*Nodding*) Such as Beech Green.

Mr Roberts When?

Mr Salisbury It might take years. It all depends on numbers, and the feelings of the managers and the parents of the school.

Rev Partridge But what about Miss Read? It is unthinkable that she should have her school taken away from her.

Mr Salisbury Miss Read's welfare is our concern, of course. There would always be a post for her in the area.

Mrs Lamb But we want her here. And we don't want our school to close.

Miss Quinn Absolutely right! People in Fairacre simply won't stand for their children being uprooted and carted away in buses.

Mr Roberts I never heard such a shocking thing in my life. The idea of our little tots being hauled off to Beech Green fair gives me the shudders.

Mrs Lamb We won't have it. We will never let Fairacre school close. (*Agreement from the other managers.*)

Mr Roberts This school has served the village for eighty odd years, and I don't see why it shouldn't serve it for another hundred.

All Managers Hear! Hear!

Mr Salisbury Well, Mr Chairman, I have noted the objections of the managers, though I must point out that no decision of any kind has been made by the divisional education committee about Fairacre school.

Rev Partridge I hope that nothing will ever happen to disturb the status quo. We are all extremely happy with our little school. We should be deeply distressed if anything were done to close it, and we rely on you to keep us informed of any developments. Now, that is the end of our business, and nothing remains for me to do other than to thank Mr Wells for coming here today.

Mr Salisbury smiles, nods his head and departs.

Mr Roberts He'd better not try any funny business with our village school, and don't you bother your head about all that nonsense, Miss Read. We're all behind you on this.

Rev Partridge Indeed we are.

Miss Quinn They closed Springbourne though. Poor Miss Davis was transferred to Caxley Secondary Modern.

Mrs Lamb It's happening more and more. My cousin's village school in the New Forest is under the threat of closure. Say they may turn the school building into some kind of community asset or some such.

Mr Roberts Took 'em years to close Springbourne. A lot can happen before they think of Fairacre again. In any case, we can all have a damn good fight over it, and I bet we'd win. The parents would be with us, that I do know.

Mrs Lamb And the whole village.

One, by one, the managers depart, only **Rev Partridge** *and* **Miss Read** *remain.*

Rev Partridge We don't seem to have gone very far with this business, but at least it's been mentioned, and I think that is a good thing. He seems a good fellow, that Mr Wells - Winchester, I mean.

Miss Read Salisbury.

Rev Partridge Salisbury, yes, Salisbury. I feel he would act honourably and not do anything without letting us know.

Miss Read So I should hope. Mr Salisbury was decidedly cagey, I thought. Oh dear, I hope to goodness nothing happens! In a way, the very fact that it could to be a long drawn - out affair makes it worse. I keep wondering if I should apply for a post elsewhere.

Rev Partridge My dear girl, you mustn't think of it. The very idea. Of course, you must stay here, and we shall all see that you do!

Miss Read I do appreciate your support, it's just this ghastly hanging about. You know, the mills of God grind slowly, but they grind exceedingly small.

Rev Partridge It isn't God's mill that's doing the grinding, it's the education office machinery, and that we must put a spoke in.

Miss Read Thank you, Vicar. I really feel I cannot discuss this wretched business anymore, not tonight at least.

Rev Partridge I quite understand. (*He pats her shoulder encouragingly.*) Good night, dear Miss Read.

The Rev Partridge *departs.* **Miss Read** *looks sadly around her classroom and gathers her things,* **Mr Willet** *appears with his broom.*

Mr Willet Just checking the coke pile. I'd have an early night if I was you. You looks a bit peaky. I hears they brought up that school closing business again at your meeting. Bit of a shock, no doubt, but you put it out of your head.

Miss Read *is too stunned to reply.*

Mr Willet (*Brandishing his broom like a rifle*) Us'll rout anyone who tries to shut our village school Miss Read, you can bet your last farthing on that! Let 'em try! Let 'em try! (*He marches off.*)

Miss Read (*To audience.*) There goes a militant Christian, but how on earth did he know what happened at the meeting? *Ah well! (She picks up the school bell and rings it)* Play time, boys and girls!

The lights fade.

End of Act One.

Act Two

Scene One

The Schoolhouse. The following week. Friday 28th October 1955.

Minnie *is sitting on a chair with a broken vase at her feet. She is rocking back and forth, occasionally throwing her skirt over her head, and displaying deplorable underwear including a pair of stockings, more ladders than fabric. She is crying and wailing in a loud high-pitched voice.* **Miss Read** *enters.*

Miss Read What on earth's the matter, Minnie? Don't cry about a broken vase. We can clear that up.

Minnie It ain't the vase!

Miss Read What is it then? (*Minnie continues to wail*)

Miss Read (*Taking hold of Minnie's shoulders*) Now stop all this hanky-panky and tell me what's wrong.

(*Minnie takes up the hem of her skirt and applies it to her eyes and nose. Snivelling the while.*)

Miss Read Come on, Minnie. Come and tell me all about it. You'll feel better.

Minnie (*Sniffing and shaking her head*) Gotter clear up this vase as what I broke.

Miss Read No, I'll do it later. (*She sits in a chair by Minnie*)

Minnie It's Ern, he's coming back.

Miss Read And you don't want him?

Minnie Would you?

Miss Read No! But can't you tell him so?

Minnie What, Ern? He'll hit me if I says that.

Miss Read Well. Get the police.

Minnie He'll hit me worse if I tells them. And he'll use the strap end of his belt.

Miss Read Are you sure he's going to come back?

Minnie He wrote to Auntie, she can read see, Miss Read, an' said his place was at my side.

Miss Read What a nerve! It hasn't been for the last few weeks, has it?

Minnie Well, it's different now. That old Mrs Fowler, she don't want 'im. She's turned 'im out.

Miss Read And when is he supposed to be coming?

Minnie Tonight, and I'm too afeard to go home. And what will Bert say?

Miss Read Bert?

Minnie (*Coyly*) My boyfriend what works up Springbourne Manor. He's the under-gardener there. He's been keeping me company. I gets lonely see. I never 'as no fun.

Miss Read What about Bert?

Minnie He'll hit him too.

Miss Read Your husband will?

Minnie Yes. Bound to. And Bert will hit 'im back, and there'll be a proper set-to. (*She looks pleased at this prospect*)

Miss Read Well, you'd better let Bert know what's happening, and he can keep away. That is, if Ern comes at all. Perhaps he's only making threats.

Minnie (*Crying again*) He'll come all right. He ain't got nowhere to sleep. I dursn't face him. He'll knock me about terrible, and the kids. What am I to do?

Miss Read You say that Mrs Pringle has the letter?

Minnie Yes, she read it out to me.

Mrs Pringle *appears in the schoolroom, duster in hand. She begins to flick the duster on Miss Read's desk.*

Miss Read She'll be in the school now. I'll go and see her while you wait here.

Minnie Thank you, Miss Read. The thing with Auntie is that when she gets in a row, she always wins!

Miss Read I know!

Mrs Pringle *begins to sing "Abide with me"*. **Miss Read** *leaves the schoolhouse and walks to the schoolroom.*

Mrs Pringle (*With one hand on her heart*) My, what a start you gave me!

Miss Read It's about Minnie. She's in tears about that husband of hers and seems afraid to go home.

Mrs Pringle I knows that. She's been no better than she should be while he's been away. Carrying on with that Bert. Ern's promised to give her a thundering good 'iding.

Miss Read But he's threatening her just because he wants somewhere to sleep. It all seems most unfair to me. After all, he left her.

Mrs Pringle Maybe. But his place is in his own home, with Minnie.

Miss Read But, he's intimidating her.

Mrs Pringle Natural, ain't it? How else did she get her last baby?

Miss Read The point is, Mrs Pringle, that it really wouldn't be safe to let her go home if he intends to come and knock her about. Should we tell the police?

Mrs Pringle What, and let the neighbours have a free show? Not likely.

Miss Read But the children…..

Mrs Pringle Are you trying to tell me what to do with our Minnie's children? I'll tell you straight, I'm not having that tribe settling on me with all I've got to do. I'm sick and tired of Minnie and her tribe, and the sooner she pushes off and faces up to the trouble she's made the better.

Miss Read So you won't help.

Mrs Pringle I've done nothing but help with that silly girl, and I'm wore out with it.

Miss Read I can understand that, and I think you've been remarkably patient. But now what's to be done?

Mrs Pringle I've been thinking about the best way to tackle this ever since I got Ern's letter. He can talk, going off with that old trollop who's old enough to be his mother.

Miss Read But, Mrs Pringle-

Mrs Pringle What I'm going to do is go back with Minnie and the kids to Springbourne and sleep the night at her place, with the rolling pin on one side of me and the poker on the other. I'll soon settle that Ern's hash if he dares to put foot inside the place. We don't need no police, Miss Read, that I can tell you!

Miss Read Splendid! Can I go and tell Minnie?

Mrs Pringle Yes. And I'll be ready in half an hour sharp, tell her, just as soon as I've set this filthy school to rights.

Miss Read *leaves the schoolroom and moves to the schoolhouse.*

Mrs Pringle *sings "Fight the Good Fight with all thy might".*

The lights fade.

Scene Two

The Schoolhouse, next afternoon. **Miss Read** *and* **Miss Clare** *are just finishing afternoon tea.*

Miss Clare I hear that since Miss Parr died last month, the manor house has been sold.

Miss Read According to Mr Willet, it's to be converted into flats.

Miss Clare How well I remember Miss Parr. She was a school manager when I first became a very inexperienced pupil-teacher.

Miss Read Yes, she appointed me to the post here too. Always a stickler for etiquette.

Miss Clare I recall she met Alice Leat in the lane, Alice Willet now. Alice was but a child of six then. Miss Parr was shocked to find that the little girl omitted to curtsy to her. At once she took the child to her mother and demanded instant punishment.

Miss Read But surely....

Miss Clare My dear, it was quite understandable. It was customary then for our children to curtsy to the gentry. Miss Parr was doing her duty, as she saw it, by correcting the child. No one questioned her action. Other days, other ways, you know. It's only now, sometimes, looking back - I wonder.

Miss Read When you say that nobody questioned the actions of his superiors, do you mean that they were automatically considered right, or what?

Miss Clare We recognised the injustice, my dear, as clearly as you do. But we bore more in silence for we had so much to lose by rebellion. Jobs were hard to come by in those days, and no work meant no food. It was as simple as that. A sharp retort might mean instant dismissal, and perhaps no reference, which might mean months, or even years without a suitable post. No wonder my poor mother's favourite maxim was "civility costs nothing". She knew, only too well, that civility meant more than that to people like us. It was a vital necessity to a wage earner when we were young.

Rev Partridge *knocks on the door.* **Miss Read** *lets him in.*

Rev Partridge Good afternoon, dear Miss Read, I do hope I'm not interrupting anything.

Miss Read Of course not, do come in vicar, come in and see an old friend.

Rev Partridge Miss Clare! How delightful to see you. I hope you are well during your retirement.

Miss Clare I am, thank you.

Rev Partridge (*A little uncomfortably*) I have received a somewhat disturbing letter from the office.

Miss Clare Would you like me to wait in the other room, if this is an important and confidential matter?

Miss Read Of course not.

Rev Partridge No, not at all, Miss Clare.

Miss Read If anyone has a right to hear news of Fairacre school, it's you. The letter, Vicar?

Rev Partridge It states, in guarded terms, the authority's medium-term policy of closing small schools which are no longer economically viable to run. It points out that our school numbers are dwindling steadily over the years, and that Mr Salisbury had touched on this matter at the last managers' meeting.

Miss Read Yes, we are down to twenty-eight.

Miss Clare (*Sadly.*) When I started teaching at Fairacre there were over a hundred on the roll.

Rev Partridge The letter goes on to make clear that nothing will be done without local consultation. Closure may never happen, should numbers increase, or other circumstances make the school viable.

Should it be deemed necessary to close Fairacre school, then the children will attend Beech Green school, the nearest neighbour.

There is a silence.

Miss Clare So there were foundations to all those rumours. There usually are.

Miss Read All this is very upsetting. I am so happy at Fairacre.

Rev Partridge And Fairacre is very, very happy with you as our Headmistress, dear Miss Read. I think we must arrange a public meeting with the village.

Miss Clare I agree.

Miss Read Yes, it is the right and proper thing to do. After all, it's not only the parents that are involved, but everyone in Fairacre. When you have agreed a date with the school managers, and, of course, Mr Salisbury, I will send out notes to the parents.

Rev Partridge Splendid! Splendid! It will be a good thing to see how the wind blows in the village. Nothing but good can come of airing our feelings, I feel sure. I will go back to the vicarage now and arrange a date for our public meeting. Miss Clare, when I've done so, may I call back here and drive you home? I must visit Beech Green to arrange poor Mr Brewer's funeral.

Miss Clare Thank you, Vicar I am most grateful.

Rev Partridge *exits.*

Miss Clare All very sad, my dear.

Miss Read It is, indeed.

Miss Clare And your own plans?

Miss Read No doubt the education authorities will offer me another post, but who knows where? Will I have to leave the schoolhouse? Oh, how I wish I had been sensible, and bought a house years ago.

Miss Clare Let's hope and pray it won't come to that. Fairacre will be very sad to see you leave.

Miss Read That's very kind, but like me, Fairacre may not have a choice! Of course, you will feel this deeply as well after forty-odd years standing under that pitched roof next door.

Miss Clare If it does happen, I imagine it will be some time before the plans all go through. I doubt if I will live to see it. (*Quietly, almost to herself*) In many ways, I hope I don't.

Miss Read But surely, you are stronger now. You look much better then when you were teaching. I sincerely hope that you'll flourish for another thirty years.

Miss Clare I've had a good life, and a useful one too, I hope. And I've loved every moment of it. But to tell you the truth, my dear, I'm getting tired now, and I shall be happy and ready to step aside whenever my time comes. I like to think of someone else teaching the children here, someone else picking my roses and sitting under the apple tree I watched my father plant. I've had my party, said my party piece, I shall be glad to give my thanks and go quietly home. I sometimes sing that bit of Handel to myself *"Art thou weary? Rest shall be thine; rest shall be thine"*.

A sound of a car horn.

Miss Clare But the party's still on, you know. That is the vicar come to take me to Beech Green. Goodbye, my dear, and thank you.

Miss Read, *deeply moved, accompanies* **Miss Clare** *to the door.*

Miss Read (*Looking along the path*) Mrs Pringle, do come in. What can I do for you? **Mrs Pringle** *enters.*

Mrs Pringle (*Thrusting a fruit cake wrapped in greaseproof paper at* **Miss Read**) I brung you a cake. I know you're not much of a cake baker. You mainly eats boughten stuff.

Miss Read Thank you, Mrs Pringle, I'm very grateful.

Mrs Pringle Well, I happened to be baking, and thought I would do a extra one for you. I likes making cakes, makes me think of King Alfred, burning the cakes and that, and fighting them Danes. Some time ago, mind you.

Miss Read Quite.

Mrs Pringle And talking of battles, I've just had one with Doctor Martin, and feels all the better for it.

Miss Read About the dieting?

Mrs Pringle That's right. Half-starved I've been all these months, as well you know, Miss Read, and fair fainting at times with weakness. And yet, to hear that doctor talk, you'd think I'd done nothing but guzzle down grub.

Miss Read I know you've been trying very hard.

Mrs Pringle Well, it all come to a head last night, as you might say. Got me on that great iron weighing machine of his, up the surgery, like some prize porker, I always feels, balancing on that contraption, when he gives a sort of shriek and yells: "*Woman, you've gone up*! *Woman*, he calls me! *Woman*, the cheek of it!

Miss Read Oh dear!

Mrs Pringle Well, I gets off his old weighing machine, pretty smartish, and I says: Don't you come calling me *Woman* in that tone of voice. You takes my money regular out of the National Health, and I'll have a bit of common courtesy, if you don't mind. And then I told him flat, that he is no good as a doctor, or I'd have been a stone lighter by now, according to his reckoning.

Miss Read I see.

Mrs Pringle He didn't like it, I can tell you.

Miss Read What did he say?

Mrs Pringle He said I never kep' to my diet. He said I was the most cantankerous patient on his list, and the best thing I could do was to forget the diet and go my own way. What's more, he had the cheek to say that for two pins he'd advise me to go to another doctor.

Miss Read Yes, what else?

Mrs Pringle Go to another doctor, but that he wouldn't wish any such troublemaker on any of his colleagues. Them was his very words. Burnt into my brain, they is! Like being branded! A troublemaker, me!

Miss Read I shouldn't let it worry you too much. You were both rather heated, I expect, and after all, Doctor Martin is only human.

Mrs Pringle That I doubt.

Miss Read Well, getting on anyway, and rather over-worked. He's probably quite sorry about it this morning.

Mrs Pringle That I can't believe. Anyway, I felt a sight better after I'd had my say and went home and cooked a lovely plate of pig's liver, bacon and chips. It really set me up after all that orange juice and greens I've been living on. Had a good night's rest too, with something in me stomach instead of wind. I woke up a different woman. Set to baking this morning. Sort of celebration, you see. Thrown off me chains at last.

Miss Read It was kind of you to include me in the celebrations.

Mrs Pringle Well, you've looked a bit peaky of late, a bit white and spiteful. Thought a cake might cheer you up. Cheerio!

Mrs Pringle *trots off with no trace of a limp.*

Miss Read (*Faintly*) Thank you, Mrs Pringle.

The lights fade. Music.

Scene Three

The schoolroom. The Public Meeting. The blackboard states Thursday 10th November 1955.

Present are **Rev Partridge, Miss Read, Mr Roberts, Mrs Lamb, Miss Quinn, Mr Willet, Mrs Pringle, Mr Salisbury, Mrs James,** and **Mrs Benson** *there is a general chatter in the room.*

Rev Partridge Well, dear people, I think we must make a start. You know why this public meeting has been called. So many people have been concerned about the possible closure of our school that the managers think it's right and proper for us to hear what is really happening, and to put our own views forward. We are lucky to have Mr Win - Mr Salisbury, from the Caxley Educational Divisional Department, to give us the official position, I know you will all speak frankly about your feelings. He will, of course answer any questions, as will I, Miss Read, and the other school managers, if we can. Mr Salisbury, perhaps you would care to outline official education policy before we go any further? (*During the scene*, **Mr Salisbury** *makes the occasional note in his book*)

Mr Salisbury Our general policy is to provide the best possible service within the money available. Now, you don't need me to tell you that times are hard, and we are all looking for the best way to stretch the limited money in the most economical way.

Mrs Benson But what about the children?

Mr Salisbury Exactly. As I was saying, we want to do our very best for the children, and we have been looking at ways and means.

Mrs Benson When's he coming to the point?

Mr Salisbury A small school, say under thirty pupils, still needs two teachers, and sometimes perhaps a third, for extra work. It needs cleaning, heating, and supplying with all the hundred and one pieces of equipment found in a school.

Mrs Pringle We knows all that. I knows it more than anybody. Years and years, I've slaved in this place.

Mr Salisbury Quite. Now, it does seem sensible to put some of these smaller schools together and make a more viable unit. There are several small schools in the area, such as Fairacre, and we think the children could benefit from being in a larger one.

Miss Quinn How will they benefit?

Mr Salisbury In a larger school, with more than twenty-eight on the role as is the case here, am I correct, Miss Read?

Miss Read (*Sadly*) Yes, twenty-eight.

Mr Salisbury In a really decent sized school, there is far more scope. Perhaps enough for the children to play football or cricket if they want to.

Miss Quinn Team sports aren't everything.

Mr Salisbury Then there is this building. That skylight letting in rain and wind for years and years.

Mr Willet Ever since I were a lad, sat in this very room. And whose fault is that. I sometimes wonder if the education people have deliberately run down the building on purpose.

Mr Salisbury Certainly not! Anyway, the building is owned by the diocese. The land is owned by the county council.

Mr Willet Every village needs its own school. Stands to reason folks wants their own children to run round the corner to school as they did. And in the end, the whole village suffers. Less and less people living in the village, taking an interest. Yank 'em off in a bus, says the higher-ups, push 'em all into one big school. It's economy we've got to think of. Economy! Economy is taking care of what you've got and making good use of it. (*He points at Mr Salisbury*) If you and the other education people think that shutting up Fairacre village school for a bit of hard cash is economy, you all wants to think about what real value means, not just money, that's the least of it, just think again and ask yourselves, what are you throwing away?

The people in the room greet this speech with loud applause and cheering. **Mr Salisbury** *looks very uncomfortable.*

Rev Partridge Are there any questions for the people here?

Mrs Lamb I've got one.

Rev Partridge Do continue, Mrs Lamb.

Mrs Lamb I agree with Mr Willet. Mr Salisbury, do you think it's right that little children should get carted off in a bus, ever so early, and back again, ever so late (in the dark, come wintertime) when they've always been used to walking round the corner to school?

Mr Salisbury I think walking round the corner to school as you put it, is the ideal way. But we don't live in an ideal way, I fear, and have to make changes.

Mrs Lamb Then if it's ideal, why change it?

Mrs Benson Ah! She's got you there!

Lots of voices raised in agreement, some general laughter.

Rev Partridge Mr Salisbury?

Mr Salisbury As I have explained, we have to do the best we can with the limited resources available.

Mrs James Mr Chairman, I am Mrs Amy James, a newcomer to Fairacre.

Rev Partridge Yes, Mrs James. What would you like to say?

Mrs James I do think that this place is an anachronism.

Miss Quinn What do you mean?

Mrs James Well, the building for a start. It's really had its time, you know. Those antiquated tortoise stoves, that ghastly sky-light forever letting in the rain and a wicked draught. It's not good enough!

General muttering of disagreement with **Mrs James** *from the others.*

Mrs Benson Speaking as a parent who had three children educated at Fairacre village school, and, who has a grandchild in Miss Read's class, I have no complaints about the school, thank you very much.

General muttering of agreement.

Mr Roberts Mr Chairman, I should like to ask Mr Salisbury about something different from the financial side. What about losing a valuable part of our village life?

Mrs Benson This school is the heart of the village, we have already lost our policeman, our village shop, half our vicar, now it looks like we may lose our school as well.

Mr Willet Yes well, we may have lost half our vicar, but us still has to pay the diocese the full parish levy.

Mrs Pringle That's quite right. We lost our duckponds too! Used to be two duckponds in Fairacre.

There are general murmurs of agreement.

Mrs Lamb It's all very upsetting.

Rev Partridge Please, please, dear people. One at a time! Now, does anyone have anything to add?

Miss Quinn Yes, what happens to Miss Read?

Mr Salisbury In the event of the village school closing, Miss Read will be offered a post nearby, and will not suffer a loss of salary, as will the other staff.

Mrs Pringle What about me? I slaved away in this school for years and years, trying to keep it clean. Even when my leg was not all it should be. Traipsing up the village street three times a day.

Mr Salisbury There will be a full consultation with you.

Mr Willet But supposing Miss Read don't want to go?

Mrs Benson Yes, and what about her house?

Mr Roberts Besides, we want her to go on teaching our children.

Mr Salisbury I can assure you that the education department have Miss Read's welfare strongly in mind.

Mr Roberts What happens to this building, if the school closes. On the wall outside of this building is a plaque. 1878 it says. 1878 the date this school was built, for the village, for this village. Nigh on eighty years!

Miss Quinn And the land, what happens to that?

Mr Willet Sold by the county council for a fortune for housing, I bet!

Miss Quinn That's right. Makes you wonder if there is a hidden agenda!

General agreement in the room.

Mr Salisbury No, no hidden agenda. As I said earlier, the building belongs to the diocese and the land to the county council. I am sure that there would be full consultation about the future use. It could be a community asset of some kind, maybe the village hall could be moved here?

Rev Partridge Most unlikely, I would suggest.

Mr Roberts It is already a community asset! What's a village school, if it's not a blasted community asset? Talk like this drives me mad!

Mrs James We live in a property that backs on to the school. We expect to be kept fully informed about future use of this land.

Mr Salisbury Yes, I am aware of that. I wish to assure you all that as yet, no definite decision has been made to close Fairacre school. Should that situation arise following the meeting of the education authority, there will be full consultation with all the interested parties. All the comments and points put forward so lucidly this evening will be considered most carefully.

Rev Partridge I think that concludes our meeting, ladies and gentlemen. Thank you for attending. May the hand of the Lord guide our path. Goodnight.

Mr Salisbury *walks out. The rest leave. There are various "good nights", see you tomorrow, wonder if that did any good? Been at this school all me schooldays, and my father afore me, won't catch me sending our two little 'uns to Beech Green, bus or no bus...*

Miss Read *is left alone with* **Mr Willet.**

Mr Willet Shall I lock up, Miss Read?

Miss Read (*Visibly upset.*) No thank you, I would like to lock the school this evening.

Mr Willet Righto! See you in the morning, bright and early.

Miss Read Yes, thank you, Mr Willet.

Mr Willet Good night, Miss.

Miss Read Good night.

Miss Read *gathers her things, looks sadly round the room, picks up the big key for the school and walks through the audience.*

The lights fade Music.

Scene Four

The schoolhouse two days later. Saturday 12th November 1955. **Miss Read** *is with* **Mrs Pringle.**

Mrs Pringle Seen the Caxley Chronicle this week yet?

Miss Read No, Minnie used it to wrap up a broken cup before I had time to look at it.

Mrs Pringle All about Arthur Coggs and them two Bryants. 'Ad up in Crown Court, for pinching that lead from Mr Mawn's and other things, like I said they would be.

Miss Read Oh dear.

Mrs Pringle Oh yes! I was right see. Like the rest of the village.

Miss Read (*Attempting to interrupt*) But Mrs Pringle…

Mrs Pringle The Bryants were sent down for three years, and Arthur Coggs got two years. Not that he'll be there all that time, more's the pity. They takes off the time he's been in custody already see.

Miss Read Yes, I know that.

Mrs Pringle And if he behaves hi'self, he'll get another few months cut off his time inside. I reckon he's been lucky this time. He'll be back in Fairacre before we can turn round.

Miss Read Well, at least he'll be kept out of the way for some time.

Mrs Pringle He'll start all over again when he does get out.

Miss Read Yes, very likely.

Mrs Pringle When I think that Arthur Coggs signed the pledge the same year as I did, it makes me fair grieve. He didn't keep that vow for long, did he? I mind his sister Ethel took the pledge on the same day. As nice a girl as you could wish to meet, with long black hair she could sit on. When it was down, I mean. All dressed in white, she was. It was her old confirmation dress, and very nice too with a crochet collar. Ethel and Arthur's old ma was a great one for crochet. Yards of it she did. Bedspreads, table cloths, nothing was too much for her, and Ethel's drawers, if you'll pardon the word, was always edged with crochet work.

Miss Read Very nice.

Mrs Pringle She went into the Caxley Co-op when she left school, the bacon counter. She married Charlie Tibble whose uncle used to sweep the High Street, if you remember, a funny old party, with a waxed moustache like the Kaiser.

Miss Read No, I don't think I ever saw him.

Mrs Pringle I was always fond of Ethel. Never deserved to have a rapscallion like that Arthur for a brother.

Miss Read No indeed.

Mrs Pringle Mind you, she's not the looker she was. Got rather fat, but she'd had two boys. And they was both ten-pounders, which don't do a woman much good, especially if she's narrow in the hips.

Miss Read Well I wouldn't know myself.

Mrs Pringle They've been in trouble too, so I hears.

Miss Read What sort of trouble?

Mrs Pringle Fighting and that, in pubs.

Miss Read So they didn't take after Ethel?

Mrs Pringle Don't look like it. Both on probation, I was told. Ah well! Bad blood will out, I always say.

Miss Read How is Mrs Coggs?

Mrs Pringle Gone to pieces. As a good neighbour, I lent her my Caxley, and I've never seen a body look so white and whey faced as what she did. Nearly fell off her chair with shock, she did.

Miss Read Wouldn't it have been kinder to tell her yourself, if she'd asked?

Mrs Pringle I didn't trust myself not to break down. A woman's heart's a funny thing, you know. She loves that man of hers even with his little failings.

Miss Read I should think little failings hardly cover Arthur Coggs' criminal activities.

Mrs Pringle I was glad to see the tears come. I said to her, that's right! A good cry will ease that breaking heart.

Miss Read Mrs Pringle, for pity's sake spare me all this sentimental mush! Mrs Coggs knew quite well that Arthur would go to prison, and she knew that he deserved it. If I were in her shoes, I'd breathe a sigh of relief.

Mrs Pringle Yes, well there's some in this parish what leads an unnatural life, so their opinions don't altogether matter.

Miss Read Thank you!

Mrs Pringle There's some 'as has no feeling heart for the misfortunes of others. It's plain to see it would be useless to come to you in trouble, and I'm glad that poor, poor, Mrs Coggs had my shoulder to cry on in her time of affliction. One of these days, you may be in the same boat.

Before **Miss Read** *can reply there is a knock on the door.* **Miss Read** *leaves and returns with* **Mr Willet**, *looking white and shaken.*

Mr Willet Just seen the Vicar. He asked me to let you know he's just got back from Beech Green.

Miss Read Oh no! Not Miss Clare? (**Mr Willet** *nods dumbly. Both* **Miss Read** *and* **Mrs Pringle** *sit down.*)

Miss Read When?

Mr Willet This morning. That kind lady next door popped in to take her up a cup of tea.

Miss Read Mrs John.

Mr Willet Yes, Mrs John. Took her up a cup of tea and found her. She thought Miss Clare was asleep, but she wasn't. Doctor Martin's been to the cottage, a straightforward case of heart failure, it was.

Miss Read I saw her last week. I went every week.

Mr Willet I know you did. Dolly looked forward to your visits.

Miss Read As I left her, she said what she always said when we parted.

Mrs Pringle (*Gently, close to tears*) What were that, Miss Read.

Miss Read Love to Fairacre, just that.

62

Mr Willet Well, we know that Fairacre meant a lot more to her than Beech Green, even though she lived there for most of her life.

Miss Read Lived in the same cottage since a little girl of six.

Mr Willet Shame she never married. I wonder if she had a sweetheart?

Miss Read Indeed she did. She was engaged to Arnold Fletcher, the only love of her life. Tragically, he did not come back from the first world war.

Mrs Pringle I never knew that.

Mr Willet Nor me.

Miss Read Not many people did.

Mrs Pringle Will the funeral be in Fairacre?

Miss Read I expect so, in Saint Patrick's. No doubt the Vicar will deal with that.

Mr Willet Doctor Martin has asked my Alice to go and lay her out, ready for the undertaker.

Miss Read and **Mrs Pringle** *nod together.*

Miss Read No one better than Mrs Willet for that sad task.

Mrs Pringle No family, of course.

Miss Read No children of her own, but I can't help thinking of the countless school children who have passed through her hands. They've a lot to be thankful for.

Mr Willet I'm going to ring the church bell, for Miss Clare. Let the parish know she's gone home. Seems right to me. (*He leaves*)

Mrs Pringle (*Upset, gazing, eyes unseeing*) Worked together with Miss Clare, I did, for years and years.

Miss Read I know you did.

Mrs Pringle She was good to me, very good.

Miss Read She was good to us all, a pleasure to work with, she'll never be forgotten.

Mrs Pringle No, she won't. Always generous at Christmas as well. See this scarf, I still wears it. Miss Clare gave it me, years ago. (*The sound of a half- muffled church bell rings*) Ah, good old Bob Willet. He'll toll that bell seventy-two times.

Miss Read One toll for every year of Miss Clare's life. "*For whom the bell tolls, it tolls for thee*".

Mrs Pringle That's right, Miss Read. (**Miss Read** *gently pats* **Mrs Pringle** *on the shoulder*)

Mrs Pringle It's sad for you, Miss Read, you were a good friend to Miss Clare.

Miss Read Yes, it's a shock too, for us all.

Mrs Pringle Yes, it is. Ah well! No good grieving over times past. I suppose we all got to go home somewhen, but somehow, that bell brings it home to you, don't it, brings it home!

Lights fade. The bell tolls louder.

Music "Miss Clare Remembers" by Enya.

Scene Five

The Schoolhouse, the following week. Friday 18th November 1955. **Minnie** *is sweeping the table with a dustpan and brush, banging very loudly.* **Miss Read** *enters.*

Miss Read You're working overtime, Minnie.

Minnie Why what's the time?

Miss Read (*Indicates the clock on the "fourth" wall*) Almost four-thirty.

Minnie (*Looking puzzled at the clock*) Oh, the clock. I never looks at the clock. I never quite got round to learning how to tell the time. It's them two hands see, they muddles me up.

Miss Read Good gracious! How do you know what time to set out from Springbourne to come here?

Minnie Bus comes. I knows when to finish here cos, I hears the kids going home. Anyway, it don't matter what time I finishes no more. Ern don't finish till five, we don't have our tea 'till then.

Miss Read Is he working at Caxley?

Minnie He's working up the manor.

Miss Read Springbourne Manor?

Minnie That's right.

Miss Read Doesn't it make things a bit awkward? I thought Bert worked there. After all they're both, er, fond of you, Minnie.

Minnie Oh, Bert's been and gone. The boss sent him packing.

Miss Read Mr Hurley did?

Minnie There's no Hurleys at Springbourne now. Mr David was the last, and he sold up to new people. Name of Potter.

Miss Read Of course! And why was Bert dismissed?

Minnie Pinchin' things. He had a regular job selling the vegetables and fruit and that, to a bloke in Caxley. Made quite a bit that way.

Miss Read I'm glad he was found out.

Minnie Oh, he wouldn't have been, but for Mrs Potter goin' into this 'ere greengrocers for some lettuces, because Bert told her there wasn't none ready for the table yet.

Miss Read What happened?

Minnie She said what lovely lettuces, and where did they come from? The man said that he'd got a lot of stuff from Springbourne

Manor, and it was always fresh, and everybody liked it. So, of course, when she come home, she faced Bert with it.

Miss Read I should think so!

Minnie A shame, really. He was doin' very nicely till then. Anyway, Mr Potter packed 'im off with a week's wages and no reference. Still, he done him a good turn really, seeing as Bert's got a job laying gas pipes across the country, and makes a mint of money.

Miss Read So Ern has got Bert's job?

Minnie That's right. Mr Potter come down to me one evening and talked about Ern coming back and settling down to be a good husband and father, and what did I think?

Miss Read And what did you say?

Minnie I said I wanted him back, as long as he didn't hit me or the kids or nothin', and as long as he behaved proper, he was lovely.

Miss Read So you've forgiven him?

Minnie Well, yes. And Mr Potter said he could have the job with free fruit and veg, as long as 'e behaved hisself. And if he didn't, I was to go and tell him, and he'd speak sharp to him.

Miss Read Well, it all seems to have worked out very satisfactorily Minnie. But look at the time! You must hurry back!

Minnie I wanted to tell you, now that Ern's back, I don't need to come out so much, and I wondered if you could manage without me?

Miss Read Manage without you? Why, of course I can , Minnie. I'm just grateful to you for helping me out these last few weeks, but of course, you need more time at home now.

Minnie I could ask my cousin, Josh, Josh Pringle to help you if you likes. Only you'd have to hide yer matches away. He's not quite all there, he loves fire see. Auntie says he's a bit of a- a- what was it? nymphomaniac too. You'd have to keep a eye on yer 'andbag.

66

Miss Read I'm sure that we needn't bother Josh, thank you, Minnie, I can manage.

Minnie That's good. I've really enjoyed comin' here. You just say if you ever wants me again.

Miss Read Oh, I will Minnie. You hurry along now.

Minnie Ta. Miss Clare's funeral on Monday aint it?

Miss Read Yes, the school will be closed in the afternoon, in her honour. An important and sad day in Fairacre.

Minnie Cheerio, Miss Read.

Miss Read Bye, bye, Minnie.

Lights fade.

Ernest *enters and places a cloth and a cross on Miss Read's Desk. The whole cast move into place, dressed in black. They sing.*

> *He who would valiant be*
>
> *Gainst all disaster,*
>
> *Let him in constancy*
>
> *Follow the Master.*
>
> *There's no discouragement*
>
> *Shall make him once relent*
>
> *His first avowed intent*
>
> *To be a pilgrim.*
>
> *(Hymns Ancient and Modern.)*

Scene Six

Monday 21st November 1955. Saint Patrick's church.

Rev Partridge I am the resurrection and the life, saith the Lord: he that believeth in me, though he were dead, yet shall he live: and whosoever liveth and believeth in me shall never die. Forasmuch as it has pleased Almighty God to take unto himself the soul of our dear sister, Dorothy Annie Clare here departed: we therefore commit her body to the ground; earth to earth, ashes to ashes; dust to dust.

(*The Book of Common Prayer*.)

Whole Cast Amen.

Miss Read A long and lovely life has ended. I am sure that many of us gathered today will share this poignant sense of loss, yet there is no need for prolonged grief. Dolly would not wish it. Dolly will be remembered by many for years to come. There are no children of her own as immediate heirs, but all the school children she taught throughout her long service have come under her wise and gentle influence. I am sure that this will shape their views and outlook for the rest of their lives. It is with gratitude not grief we will remember her.

In memory of my dear friend and colleague, Dolly Clare.

When I am gone, fear not to say my name,

Nor speak of me in muted tones as if it were a shame for one to die.

Let me figure in your daily talk.

Tell of my loves and hates , and how I used to laugh or take a walk.

This way you'll keep me in your memory,

Which is my hope of immortality.

(*Clemance Dane*.)

The cast move off leaving **Miss Read** and **Rev Partridge** alone.

A lone voice sings:

Lord, now lettest thou thy servant depart in peace: according to thy word.

For mine eyes have seen: thy salvation;

Which thou hast prepared: before the face of all people;

To be a light to lighten the Gentiles: and to be the glory of thy people Israel.

Glory be to the Father, and to the Son, and to the Holy Ghost;

As it was in the beginning, is now. and ever shall be: world without end. Amen.

(*Book of Common Prayer.*)

Running through this canticle, we hear the children singing "One man went to mow a meadow".

Miss Read Thank You Vicar.

Rev Partridge A fitting service, I think.

Miss Read Yes, it was. (*She looks in her handbag and takes out a silver pocket watch on a chain*) I was asked by Dolly several times to give you this. It was given to her father on his retirement. He left it to Dolly, and she always kept it on the little table by her bed. It's an excellent timekeeper. She hoped you would find a use for it. (*She hands it to* **Rev Partridge**)

Rev Partridge (*Too moved to speak for a while*) How generous of her. I shall always treasure it. I've always wanted a pocket watch, but never felt I should indulge myself. This is doubly welcome - a remembrance of dear Dolly, though she would be remembered well enough without it, as you know - and something I've always wished for.

Miss Read It would have pleased her to know you like it. (*She takes out from her handbag a gold locket*) I wished I had found this earlier; I should have put it in the coffin with her.

Rev Partridge (*Taking the locket and opening it*) A tiny photograph and a lock of bright red hair. Arnold?

Miss Read Arnold. The only man she ever loved.

Rev Partridge Ah well! As Willet would say, life goes on!

Miss Read Yes indeed. I suppose we now await the letter from Mr Salisbury.

Rev Partridge Yes. I telephoned the Caxley office last week. He told me I will receive a letter shortly with the decision of the education authority. In the event of the very worst happening, what will you do?

Miss Read Confidentially, at least I don't have to worry about a home now, if I lose the schoolhouse.

Rev Partridge Miss Clare?

Miss Read Yes, she told me some time ago that she was leaving her cottage to me in her will.

Rev Partridge So kind of her.

Miss Read Yes, I am overwhelmed by her generosity.

Rev Partridge And your other plans?

Miss Read I am thinking about maybe leaving the teaching profession, if I am forced to do so. Over the years I've had one or two short articles published in the Caxley Chronicle. I may even write about the life of a village schoolmistress! Heavily disguised, of course! (*To audience*) If I were to take up writing my own memoirs, I ought to think of a title. "*Memories of a Village Schoolteacher*"? Too dull. "*Rooks Above the Playground*"? Too fanciful. "*Country Children*", "*The Heart of the Village*"? No, not right.

Rev Partridge I pray earnestly that it won't come to that!

Miss Read Well, to quote Mr Asquith, "*We must wait and see*".

The lights fade. **Miss Read** *and* **Rev Partridge** *leave together.*

Music: Young children singing "Away in a manger".

Scene Seven

The Schoolroom last day of the Christmas term. The blackboard states Friday 16th December 1955.

Miss Read (*Picking up the school bell and ringing it*) Home time, boys and girls. (*The sound of children leaving the school*)

Miss Read (*Waving*) Goodbye children. Straight home now. Merry Christmas!

The Pupils Merry Christmas, Miss Read.

The Rev Partridge (*arrives with the letter*) Goodbye children, Merry Christmas.

The Pupils Merry Christmas, sir.

Rev Partridge Don't forget to help your mothers at Christmas.

The Pupils (*Cheekily*) You too sir!

Miss Read Ernest, just a minute. (*She picks up a homemade tinsel star and hands it to him*)

Ernest Thanks Miss. Is our school truly going to shut?

Miss Read I don't know yet. I hope not.

Ernest I hopes not, too (*He holds the star at arms-length*) Good, ain't it?

Miss Read Very good. (**Ernest** *leaves*)

Rev Partridge Dear, dear, children, every one of them. Particularly the poor Coggs children.

Miss Read Yes, they are. As for Joe, well, life has not been kind to him yet. He's a quick learner despite his chaotic upbringing. I have great hopes for his future. Is this the letter?

Rev Partridge Yes, it is. It arrived with the afternoon post at the vicarage. I think it best if I let you read it alone, Miss Read.

Miss Read Very well. Have you read it? (**The Rev Partridge** *nods. He touches* **Miss Read** *gently on the arm and leaves) There is the soundscape of the village.*

Miss Read *pauses, takes a deep breath and opens the letter and reads it. She takes a long look around the schoolroom, picks up the letter and carefully folds it. She moves to the blackboard cleans it and writes on it "The End". She picks up the school key and walks very slowly through the audience. There is the sound of a heavy door closing and a lock being turned.*

END

Furniture and Property Lists

ACT ONE

On Stage

Stage Right - School house.

Kitchen table, two wooden kitchen chairs.

Small Cupboard. In it 2/3 Cups and saucers.

Stage Left – School room.

1950s Teacher's desk and chair. On desk and school hand bell. Set of keys. In desk drawer; sewing – 2 gingham aprons, 2 hankies.

Blackboard on easel, white chalk, duster. 4/5 chairs in the audience area for children. School writing book and pencil on each child's chair.

Personal

Enamel bucket and wooden scrubbing brush. (Mrs Pringle)

"Cat" in an old blanket. (Earnest)

Fragments of an old paint brush. (Mrs Pringle)

Written list of Hymns. (Rev Partridge)

Tray with coffee cups, coffee pot, cream jug, chocolate biscuits. (Miss Read)

Black oilcloth bag containing a cabbage. (Mrs Pringle)

Tea towel. (Dr Martin)

Dr's Bag. (Dr Martin)

Envelope containing a cheque. (Rev Partridge)

Bunch of Garden Flowers. (Linda)

Tea tray with tea pot, milk jug, sugar and teacups. (Miss Read)

Pound Note. Four marbles, a stub of a pencil, a lump of bubble gum, a jagged piece of red glass. (Earnest)

Tea cloths in Black oilcloth bag. (Mrs Pringle)

Large Broom (Mr Willet)

Children's' exercise books. (Miss Read)

Notebook and pen. (Salisbury)

Large broom- as before (Mr Willet)

ACT TWO

On Stage – as before. On Miss Read's desk, homemade tinsel star.

Personal

Broken Vase. (Minnie)

Duster. (Mrs Pringle)

Tea tray, as before. (Miss Read)

Black oilcloth bag with cake wrapped in greaseproof paper. (Mrs Pringle)

Notebook and pen, as before. (Salisbury)

Dustpan and brush. (Minnie)

Cloth/sheet to cover Miss Read's desk. Wooden Cross. (Earnest)

Book of Common Prayer. (Rev Partridge)

School book with poem hand-written. (Miss Read)

Silver pocket watch and chain. (Miss Read)

Gold locket on a chain – opening. (Miss Read)

Brown envelope containing letter. (Rev Partridge)

The following plays by Ron Perry,
adapted from Miss Read's Thrush Green books,
are available through Amazon.

MISS READ'S THRUSH GREEN

adapted for the stage by Ron Perry

ISBN 9781727772760

MISS READ REMEMBERED

a play by Ron Perry

ISBN 9781095527894

MISS READ'S RETURN TO THRUSH GREEN

adapted for the stage by Ron Perry

ISBN 9798648549050

Printed in Great Britain
by Amazon